THE
ABORTION
WOUNDED
CHURCH

Developing a Culture of Healing
for the Abortion Wounded

KAREN A. ELLISON

PRESIDENT, DEEPER STILL

HIGH BRIDGE BOOKS
HOUSTON

Contents

Letter to the Reader

Dear Christian Leader,

Thank you for taking the time to further inform your heart and mind about the role of the Church in healing women and men with abortion wounded hearts. These wounds are often hidden from plain sight, but they are immense and deep. Healing those with abortion wounded hearts is essential to ending abortion and for bringing restoration to the lives of individuals and families impacted by abortion. Your voice and influence cannot be underestimated. If we are going to turn the tide from a culture of death to a culture of life, and from a culture of shame to a culture of healing and freedom, then it's the Lord's Church that will lead the charge. Thank you for answering the call.

For a deeper understanding of the abortion wounded heart please get a copy of my book—*Healing the Hurt that Won't Heal: Freedom for the Abortion-Wounded and Help for the Church They Fear*.

Until all are healed,
Karen A. Ellison, President
Deeper Still

Introduction

Maybe you shouldn't be so hard on yourself." These were the words I heard coming from the pastor I had just confessed my abortion to and to whom I had just poured out my heart. His response initially left me feeling stunned. I'm sure I had a puzzled look on my face.

But within seconds, I could feel my soul shrinking back like a wave that recedes from the shore. I was expectant or hopeful that my desperate heart would receive some profound morsel that would have satisfied my hunger for relief. But what I got felt like a sip of sugar water.

It had been a couple of months since my abortion, and I was trying to process it all internally by myself. I would have liked to bring a friend or spiritual authority into my inner world, but I didn't know who or how. Plus, I was aware of this cloud of shame that was now overshadowing my mother. She was fighting her own battle and was feeling responsible for my every internal tear. She and I did not talk much about it during those days. I was trying to protect her, and she was trying to protect me, so we mostly kept our tormenting secrets to ourselves.

I knew my mother was seeking spiritual and emotional relief because she would call 1-800 prayer lines. She would pour out her heart to strangers over the phone, who would pray for her. I was thankful that she did that, but it also showed me how desperate her struggle was to get relief from the guilt, shame, and responsibility she was carrying. It was my mother who suggested that we go talk to a pastor together. I didn't object, but at that time I was doing it more for her than for myself. She made an appointment with a pastor several towns away.

It takes a lot of emotional willpower to pour out your story to a stranger. But when it's a pastor, you have certain expectations that he will give you the words of life that your desperate soul needs to hear. Now, in this man's defense, my mother and I had no relationship with this clergyman. Our shame-filled, abortion-wounded hearts would not dare seek out a spiritual shepherd that knew us or was invested in our spiritual health. We took the cowardly path of anonymity, hoping we would find the words of life we needed from a random man with a collar.

After he told me I shouldn't be so hard on myself, he then said that the church (referring to his denomination) had not yet taken a position on abortion. The implication was that abortion is a gray area, so don't jump to any self-condemning conclusions until we get this thing figured out. I was a 22-year-old heartbroken young lady, grieving and feeling as if I'd forfeited all the good things God had for me in life, but in that moment, I felt as if I should turn the table and be the one to minister to this pastor and help him understand what abortion really is and what it does to people. I believe he was a good and caring man. I believe he heard my story and was filled with compassion for me. And he in no way condemned me or tried to put any legalistic yoke upon me. But he also didn't see my deepest need, nor did he know how to speak to it. For me to hear that I shouldn't be so hard on myself was like a man of God telling me that "the blood stain on your hands was really not that bad, and yes, you've been through something hard but you're young and you have your whole life in front of you, so don't fret; it's going to be okay."

So why didn't those words satisfy? What did I need to hear from that shepherd that day? I believe I simply needed to hear and be convinced of this: that the blood shed by the Lord Jesus Christ on the cross was sufficient to pay my debt and that His blood speaks louder than the blood of my children that cries out from the ground. It's that truth that will lift the yoke of bondage, set the captive free, and will breathe new life into a deflated soul.

Receiving that truth would not have been the end of my healing journey, but it certainly would have been a beginning. When those of us who were once abortion-wounded were able to lay hold of that foundational truth, then we could at least accept that God had pardoned us and that He had released us from our prison of guilt and shame. His grace and mercy take on a new reality for us when we experience its power and when we can see PAID IN FULL stamped over our certificate of debt.

A recent study released by LifeWay Research in November 2015 (lifewayresearch.com) reveals that 70% of American women who have abortions identify themselves as Christian.

Years later, after I'd experienced much healing and by God's grace gained the ability to minister to others, the Lord revealed that He still had more for me. I was discovering that there is always a fresh revelation that can bring another layer of healing that takes you deeper still.

I once confessed my abortion to a Catholic priest. It's not that I did not feel thoroughly forgiven and pardoned from the Lord, because I did, and it's not that I felt like I was still holding unforgiveness toward anyone, because I felt like all those relationships had been reconciled. Still, I felt the prompting of the Holy Spirit to confess my abortion to him. In response, he said several good things, but one phrase pierced my heart. He said, "Karen, as a representative and on behalf of the body of Christ, I declare that we forgive you." Try to imagine how that hit me. I know that the Bible teaches that we are members of one another and that when one suffers, we all suffer, but I had never considered or been in a context where I could ask the body of Christ to forgive me for how my sin affected them and our collective conscious. But the Lord sent me this priest to release a word of forgiveness to me on behalf of the family of God and the body of Christ. Now that was a morsel that satisfied my soul.

The Abortion Wounded Church

So why do I use the term abortion-wounded church? Even though it's impossible to get statistics that tell the whole story, a recent study released by LifeWay Research in November 2015 (lifewayresearch.com) reveals that 70% of American women who have abortions identify themselves as Christian.[3] This includes broad definitions of Catholics, Protestants, Evangelical, Charismatic, Fundamentalist, and Non-Denominational. It is impossible to know the true faith of these women's hearts, but something in their lives makes them identify themselves as God-believing or as part of His Church. In my case, I was certainly one of those statistics. Even though these statistics cannot tell us everything we would like to know, they do reveal enough to be alarming. That same study also revealed that 76% of those taking the survey said that local churches had no influence on their decision to abort.[4]

If you are a pastor, priest, clergy, chaplain, or lay leader, I hope these statistics are disturbing to you. How can these numbers be so high? Why is there seemingly so little differentiation between Christian and non-Christian American women and men choosing to abort their children? Why does the church have so little influence in our culture regarding life and death choices for unborn children? Where is the disconnect? My prayer is that these questions would cause you to wrestle not just with the *why* but would lead you to ask *what* does the Lord want me to do?

Seventy-six percent of those taking the survey said that local churches had no influence on their decision to abort.

The struggle for the abortion-wounded parishioner is not just that they live with their own secret torment, but they avoid serving at church except in ways that are non-threatening. You see, it makes her anxious to be around children, so she can't serve in children's church. He or she can't help chaperone a youth group trip because he or she worries about what they'll do if students start asking about sex or one of them confesses to having an abortion. It's too risky to join a home fellowship group because participants might be asked to share their testimonies, and that is too vulnerable. When you're still in bondage to your abortion wounds, your plan is to stay silent, behave yourself, don't cause problems, and hope no one asks too many questions. A heart in that condition can only embrace your church's mission and vision intellectually and from the comfort of their back-row pew.

Spiritual Forces

Even though I had a core conviction that abortion was wrong and was taking the life of a baby, other influences and pressures were strong enough to cause me to consent to the thing I said I was against. Let me address at least two of those spiritual forces that make people vulnerable to abortion in spite of their stated view on abortion.

There are real spiritual forces that can feel more over-powering than your convictions and conscience. Fear is certainly one of them, and deception is the other. A spirit of fear will fuel a lie and make it global ("It will ruin my whole life"). It's non-specific and is always full of hopelessness. Deception, on the other hand, can sound reasonable, practical, and even wise ("I'm too young and immature to have a baby"). These influences don't require that you have faith in God or that you would need the help of others. In fact, you can get an abortion on your own, and no one else has to know or be involved.

As with all lies, they are just that—lies that will betray you. It's just like what the White Witch said to Edmund in *The Lion, The Witch, and The Wardrobe:* "I'm a witch, fool. A witch doesn't have to keep promises. All she has to do is make them."

When these spiritual forces of fear and deception are coupled with human pride and rebellion, they gain control to overpower your soul. As a shepherd and spiritual authority, you cannot make someone repent of their pride and rebellion, but you can at least address those strongholds in people's lives through your preaching, teaching, and counseling.

As a shepherd and spiritual authority over your flock, and in conjunction with your church leadership and intercessors, you can spiritually address spirits of fear and deception. You can pray to bind them up in the name of Jesus in order to mitigate their influence on your flock. You can also loose the blessing of the spirit of truth, peace, and a sound mind upon your congregation (Matthew 16:18–19). This spiritual weapon of warfare carries tremendous weight and power to clear the spiritual air around the individuals and families in your care.

There could be many families in your congregation dealing with a crisis pregnancy situation who are going to make decisions one way or another about the life of a baby, even if they don't plan on ever telling you. The 2015 study sited earlier by LifeWay Research revealed that 43% of women who have had an abortion were attending a Christian church once a month or more at the time of one of their abortions.[5]

If you are a pastor, my hope is that you will take encouragement in this: Your influence, both through your teachings and through the corporate intercession of your leadership, will make a difference in the decisions people make, even if it's without your knowledge. You and your leaders can create a safe environment for your lambs to be rescued from the thicket if you bring forth the hard truth about abortion and couple it with your shepherding heart of love, mercy, and grace.

Forty-three percent of women who have had an abortion were attending a Christian church once a month or more at the time of one of their abortions.

At the completion of our Deeper Still retreats, we give our participants a letter addressed to their pastor. This letter describes the healing journey they have just been through in this retreat, and it invites their spiritual leader into their ongoing spiritual health and growth. This letter helps to break the ice between the participant and their pastor. It is also intended to help the pastor affirm this new season of healing, wholeness, and integration into the body. *I cannot overstate how significant a pastor's invitation and affirmation will be in this person's life as they find their place in the body.*

Here are a few examples from those who have trusted God enough to make an appointment with their pastor and bring him into their story.

Pat shares:

> At the end of the retreat, you handed us the letter to give to our pastor. I immediately cringed in fear. Throughout the following week, I wondered if I really dared to speak openly and honestly to my pastor. Our new pastor was only 28 years old and fresh into ministry. I wondered would he understand? Would he reject me? Would he place judgment on me?
>
> That next Sunday I handed him the letter with trembling hands and a crackling voice. "Don't read it now," I said. "Read it next week, and then we'll talk." My anxiety level increased throughout the week as I anticipated his response. When the day approached, I was a nervous wreck. My husband and I met in his office. I began telling him my story. At one point he just put his head on the desk and started to groan. The thought entered my mind that he was going to reprimand me—then what would I do? But just the opposite took place. Instead of rejection, judgment, or criticism, he responded with tears of joy. He shook his head

and affirmed how richly God's mercy and grace had been poured out to us.

Our church is composed of many people who are living with addictions, homelessness, and other life-wounding hidden issues. He asked us to be part of the leadership team that would reach out to those who were wounded and hopeless. We knew our transparency would be key in building that trust with others. My husband and I knew it was time to share our abortion-recovery story with a larger group. We spoke on SOHL Sunday (Sanctity of Human Life Sunday). In the past this had been a Sunday we would skip. It was too painful. This year we shared how God patiently waits to redeem us and bring us into full reconciliation and restoration. The response was overwhelming and far greater than we could have imagined. Many men and women confessed to their abortions and other devastating dark secrets. The next week we continued praising God and confessing sin with one another. The Holy Spirit broke through and did amazing healing because of the Deeper Still letter telling me to go meet with my pastor.

In Sue's experience, she shared with two different pastors, and there was quite a contrast between the two. The first was the senior pastor of a large church where she is a member. She described it as a positive experience.

Sue shares:

He was genuine and interested in hearing my story. He made good eye contact and I did not feel rushed. However, he seemed a little perplexed, as if he wasn't really aware of this problem in the church, but it was as if he wasn't sure how he would handle it if it did come up. But still, he seemed appreciative of the time to hear from me and learn new insights.

In contrast though, she made an appointment with a former pastor from a church she used to attend in another state, while on vacation.

Sue shares:

He sat and listened but seemed a little guarded. At one point, he interrupted me and said, "I hate to burst your bubble, but I've never counseled with anybody who's had an abortion." I assured him that he had but he just didn't know it. I briefly shared my story. He didn't have much to say after that. He's never brought it back up to me or asked me any questions. It was awkward and emotionally unsatisfying.

Abortion Fatigue

Let's take a deeper look into what has weakened the influence of the church regarding the sanctity of human life and what can be done to gain it back.

I think it's worth acknowledging that one of the reasons abortion has become part of the landscape of our culture is because it's not an obvious moral sin for many people. We as a people, a culture, and a church have become so dull of heart when it comes to our spiritual and moral sensibilities that we either can't discern the truth that abortion is the shedding of innocent human blood, or we don't think it matters that much to God. We have a spiritual condition the Bible calls hardness of heart. As a post-Christian culture, we do not fear God nor particularly care about what He thinks about things. We have a severe case of abortion fatigue.

We are so weary of hearing about abortion and talking about abortion that it has become like abortion white noise, and we've learned to tune it out. It reminds me of a nature phenomenon that happens every summer in East Tennessee. Every July the cicadas have a "coming out" party, and you can't avoid it—at least at first. They make this shrill, piercing vibrating noise. It's loud, distracting, and it reminds me of a soundtrack from an alien movie. When this constant chorus is new, it's deafening and hard to ignore. But after a few weeks, you develop an ability to tune it out. It becomes part of the sounds of summer and you learn to live with it.

One of the reasons abortion has become part of the landscape of our culture is because it's not an obvious moral sin for many people.

I think we've learned to do the same thing with abortion. It has become the never-ending, numbing drone of our media culture. The whole discussion gets reduced to ten-second sound bites and three-minute talking points. It has become the background noise of the culture of death. With time, you adapt to it and accept it as part of the way it is. Tragically, the enterprises of media and academia have gained more authority to frame the abortion issue than the Lord's Church.

Once you become abortion weary, you look for other less controversial issues to champion. Not that God isn't impassioned about every issue that is morally egregious, but every moral transgression has its roots in the rejection of the sanctity, dignity, and protection of human life. The truth is we live in an abortion-weary world, and at some point, there's going to be an abortion-weary tipping point. We, the Church, are going to be tempted to give in and give ourselves over to the culture of death that is permeating our thinking and numbing our souls.

Several denominations already have either given up on addressing the issue or worse, some have joined the ranks of abortion advocates and have begun to perform blessing ceremonies at abortion clinics. I know of some churches who have established a fund to pay for abortions for those in need.

When I feel myself growing weary (and believe me I have those moments) there are at least two go-to verses for me.

> But they who wait for the Lord shall renew their strength; they shall mount up with wings like eagles; they shall run and not grow weary; they shall walk and not faint. (Isaiah 40:31)

And let us not grow weary in doing good, for in due season we will reap, if we do not give up. (Galatians 6:9)

We've Got to Talk about It

Not only are we tired of hearing about abortion, but we don't want to talk about it either. In fact, we don't even like to say the word. Think about it for a minute. When you say the word *abortion*, how does it make you feel? Say it several times in a row. Is it a word you just don't want to say to people? I have a theory. I think even the word abortion has a built-in curse on it. The word itself leaves a bad taste in your mouth. It has an ick factor, and if we can avoid saying it, we will. We would rather use a more euphemistic word if we must refer to abortion.

But in contrast, consider the word *adoption*. Say it several times. How does it make you feel?

It's not a word you feel you need to mask. In fact, adoption has a life-affirming feel to it.

(I'm not suggesting that adoption is not painful or that it doesn't require healing too, because it does). But adoption is God's idea and intended to be a life-giving provision. When your kids ask you what the word *adoption* means, you don't mind saying the word or explaining what it means. But who wants to tell their kids about abortion when they ask what it means?

Until we muster the courage to say the word *abortion* and then clearly define what it is, we're going to let the conspiracy of silence speak louder than the painful truth be-hind abortion. And if church leadership is not talking about it, trust me, your people aren't going to talk about it either. The 2015 LifeWay Research study indicates that 52% of churchgoers who've had an abortion haven't told anyone in their church.[6]

When you demonstrate that abortion is a word we will not cower to in this church and that this church is not only going to be a safe place to talk about abortion but a safe place to heal from abortion, then you are becoming a change agent.

Again, if I may speak to my brothers and sisters who are clergy. I fully acknowledge that you have a tough job. You want to speak the truth in love, but it's hard to know how to do that when, statistically speaking, maybe a third of the women and men in your congregations have been involved with abortion in one way or another. Because no matter how lovingly and grace-filled you try to address the subject of abortion, the truth is that many cannot hear it. People with abortion-wounded hearts have a grid of con-demnation and shame, and everything they hear about abortion gets filtered through that grid. And trust me, they are squirming in their seats even if they appear unphased on the outside.

But here's my encouragement—please don't choose to avoid it because some may not yet receive your grace. You can expose that it's the strongholds of shame and condem-nation that keep them bound and unable to confess their sin and receive redemption and healing. When we're wounded, we let those strongholds define how we hear the message of salvation, forgiveness, and deliverance. Sometimes just calling out the elephants in the room will cause those elephants to bow before the powerful name of Jesus Christ.

The 2015 LifeWay Research study indicates that 52% of churchgoers who've had an abortion haven't told anyone in their church.

When you demonstrate that *abortion* is a word we will not cower to in this church and that this church is not only going to be a safe place to talk about abortion but a safe place to heal from abortion, then you are becoming a change agent. Next, ask your congregation to put away their own sense of taboo about talking about abortion and be committed to becoming a caring and healing community. These shifts will begin to change the atmosphere regarding abortion and the rules of the engagement.

A Theology of Life

For the church to turn the tide on the culture of death, we need to make the theology of the sanctity of human life part of our core doctrinal orthodoxy. The sanctity of human life should not be considered a fringe doctrine, or a specialized side issue you are obligated to address once a year on Sanctity of Human Life Sunday. We need to normalize it as part of basic Christian discipleship and service. This means the church needs to help us develop a mindset for the sanctity of human life. To value human lives is to value image bearers of God. We are the pinnacle of His creation. He died for us to have eternal life. He did not die a criminal's death on the cross for the endangered spotted owl in your forest (nothing against spotted owls, but they do not have the same status as image bearers of God).

Dear pastor, we sincerely need to hear from you—but not just you—we need to hear from your elders, those gatekeepers who guard the orthodoxy and doctrines of the church. When they weigh in, it matters. The sanctity of human life needs to be in your Sunday School curriculum. Because even though it's hard to imagine right now, in ten years some of your fourth graders are going to be getting girls pregnant, and those girls are going to be getting abortions. Even though they learned that Jesus came in the form of a baby wrapped in swaddling clothes, they missed that God sends all His children to earth through the womb of a woman, and that He declares this creation good. Are your youth pastors and your young adult pastors openly addressing the sanctity of human life and human sexuality?

Are these truths and teachings permeating every sphere of your church culture?

To value human lives is to value image bearers of God.
We are the pinnacle of His creation.

If your strategy has been to delegate your pro-life messaging to the few pro-lifers in your congregation, then it will always be viewed as a fringe ministry. A disturbing segmenting has developed in the Church over the years. You have your Christians, and then you have your pro-life Christians. This ought not to be. Some are particularly gifted for and specifically called to certain pro-life out-reaches, but as far as how we identify ourselves, what we teach, our discipleship models, and the ways we serve and give our finances, we should be weaving an open and life-affirming culture within the entire fabric of our faith community.

If you as spiritual leaders embrace these things, then you will begin to see women and men start to come out of the closet and trust you for help. It will start with a few, but when they gain their healing, then they will get their heart back and then their voice back, and once they get their voice, they will be able to expose the truth behind abortion and the lies that keep people bound.

Consider these verses:

> I have told the glad news of deliverance in the great congregation; behold, I have not re-strained my lips, as you know, O Lord. I have not hidden your deliverance within my heart; I have spoken of your faithfulness and your sal-vation; I have not concealed your steadfast love and your faithfulness from the great congrega-tion. (Psalm 40:9–10)

I remember the first time I shared my abortion healing testimony in a church service. It was a huge milestone not only in the sense that it was good for my own soul, but I witnessed how the Lord used my restored voice and healed heart to encourage others that God can forgive, deliver, heal, and set captives free. My simple testimony of God's faithfulness started a chain reaction of others coming out of the dark and into the light.

In my case, that experience didn't start by me going to my pastor and asking him if I could share my testimony (although I would do that now). Back then, I was still too timid to initiate such a thing, but that pastor came to me. I had shared my story with him at an earlier time, and he could discern that I was healed enough that he could entrust my voice to his congregation. He took a step of faith, and I took a step of faith, and God honored it in a big way.

When captives get set free, it's not just that they have a powerful testimony to share, but it's also that they are free to begin to serve in the church from a new place of authenticity, peace, and joy. They can become useful vessels in the Lord's house and fruitful vines in His vineyard. But when their hearts are still bound by underlying guilt, shame, and grief, then much of their service is driven by performance and the need to prove something to you, God, themselves, and others.

The End-Time Bride

I am fully convinced and convicted that when abortion-wounded men and women who are Christ followers accept the Lord's invitation to go deeper still in their journey to healing and lasting freedom, then we will see an army arise. This army will be made up of mighty warriors who can advocate for the lives of unborn children. But at present, that segment of the Bride of Christ considers itself unfit for the end-time church adventure. She believes that the glorious end-time in-gathering of the saints yet to be saved will be the inheritance of more worthy Christians. But I am confident that this soon and coming Bridegroom is fiercely committed not only to her redemption, but He will do anything to gain her affections and trust. He is coming for a bride without spot or wrinkle, and He will rescue her from the vicious pimp that stole her away and then enslaved her.

When she regains her identity and gets her voice back, she will become empowered to take up the charge for those who can't speak for themselves. Right now, most of this army is like the living dead. This Bride needs shepherds who will recognize that she has been taken captive and enslaved by another master. She may be sitting in the pew every Sunday morning, and he may be serving as a Sunday morning greeter, but their sense of personal destiny and contribution in the things of God and His Kingdom are superficial.

Reach across the Denominational Aisle

We all know there is strength in numbers, and strength will grow if you initiate prayer and dialogue with other clergy in your sphere of influence. If you could share with other pastors how you've made headway in your congregation, perhaps it would give them the courage to take similar steps.

The bigger your city, the more abortion clinics you have, and therefore the more abortion-wounded you have in your city and in your churches. Would you put it on your calendar twice a year to meet some fellow clergymen outside one of the abortion clinics in town just to pray on-site? Corporate prayers from local shepherds who gather in agreement and repentance for the shedding of innocent blood on their land begins to shake the heavenlies and strikes fear into the principalities of murder and immorality over your cities. This is one way you can begin to take back the ground lost to the spirit of child sacrifice.

I was hosting a pastor's luncheon one time, and after our presentation, I asked if there were any questions or comments. We wanted to encourage these leaders in any way we could regarding their knowledge, influence, and strategies for developing a culture of life and healing in their churches or ministries. There were several seconds of silence, then finally one pastor spoke up and simply asked for one thing. He asked for even one other pastor to join him at least once when he prays in front of the Planned Parenthood across the street from his church. He said it's a lonely place to stand alone praying in front of a clinic of death.

Spiritual Warfare

I don't want to leave any impression that taking steps to turn the tide on the culture of death and developing a culture of life and healing in your church is going to be quick or without cost. In fact, it's going to be long, hard, and at great cost. The spiritual forces that fuel sexual immorality, child sacrifice, and the subsequent torment of the souls of those involved are some of the most viscous forces I've ever witnessed or encountered. You must seek God for His strategy, wisdom, power, and timing. But do not lose sight of this truth: greater is He who is in you than he who is in the world! Amen!

Deeper Still would have never gotten off the ground or flourished like it has if it weren't for the supernatural power and intervention of Jesus Christ, who is calling His church into this battle with Him. We have built this ministry on the sure foundation blocks that God revealed were necessary for walking in victory. We have been diligent to establish a culture of worship and intercession. We invest in our city by praying a blessing over it and its leaders. We pray a blessing over our city's churches; we honor and seek relational favor with them. We are diligent to preserve the unity within our teams, and we stay under the authority and protection of our board of directors and our individual spiritual shepherds. All these spiritual disciplines help maintain a huge and thick wall of Holy Spirit fire around us. We place ourselves in the shelter of the Most High, and we abide under the shadow of the Almighty. These are all magnificent provisions from the God of angel armies.

Encouragement to Pastors

It is not my intent to impose a man-made yoke on the Lord's Church or on His shepherds. You are a tremendous blessing and provision to the Church. But if the Lord has given me a voice for anything, it is for this issue. The effects of abortion and all its hellish tentacles and ripples will not be overcome if the Lord's Church will not get involved.

If you are a pastor or ministry leader who has an abortion-wounded heart, you won't have victory over the enemy's accusations unless you receive your own healing. The enemy will dog you and blackmail you for the rest of your life unless you stop running and turn around and face your accuser with the blood of the lamb and the word of your testimony. If you come into the light and model the journey to healing and freedom, then you will open the door for millions of abortion-wounded Christians to step into the light and trust Jesus for their redemption, salvation, deliverance, and healing.

If you are a pastor or ministry leader who has never been personally touched by abortion, please don't conclude that you have nothing to bring to this table. It is you the abortion-wounded fear the most. One word of rejection or condemnation from you can reinforce all the lies they ever believed about "the Church," and you will never see or hear from them again. We need to hear your heart that you do not view us as second-class or "no-class" Christians but that you, too, believe that the blood of Jesus is enough to set us free from sin and death.

The Church in every generation has had its defining battles to fight and its causes to champion. In this 21st century, the sanctity of human life is surely one of these defining issues. Will He find us faithful? Will you speak up for those who can't speak for themselves? Will you bind up the brokenhearted and proclaim liberty to the captives and freedom to those in prison? Will you give them beauty for ashes, oil of gladness for mourning, and the garments of praise instead of a spirit of fainting?

Let us rejoice and exult and give Him the glory,
for the marriage of the Lamb has come, and His
Bride has made herself ready. (Revelation 19:7)

If we lock arms, together we can prepare this Bride for
her Bridegroom.

Action Steps

Here's a summary of some action steps for those in church
leadership that can begin to change the tide of silence and
apathy within the Church:

- Develop a strategy for regularly teaching and
  preaching about the sanctity of human life and
  include it in your Sunday school curriculum.

- Cultivate a culture of worship and intercession
  so you can hear God's heart concerning the issue of abortion and His strategy for victory and
  healing.

- Address the spiritual forces of fear, condemnation, and deception.

- Create a safe environment for abortion to be
  discussed in productive and redemptive ways.

- Establish resources for healing abortion-
  wounded hearts.

- Remove the stigma of fear that would prevent someone from talking with you and confessing his or her sin.

- Reach across denominational lines to encourage and learn from other pastors; meet to pray and dialogue about establishing a culture of life and healing.

- Be willing to share your own journey and to receive deeper healing for yourself.

- Partner with at least one other pastor and go pray in front of an abortion clinic at least once a quarter and see what happens in your heart.

- Share this book with other church leaders to encourage them to action.

Concluding Thoughts

Thank you for taking the time to read and consider these thoughts and actions steps. Healing the abortion wounded heart is not just a compassionate response to those wounded by abortion it is essential. It is essential for bringing spiritual, emotional, and relational health to the abortion wounded in your church. And it is also essential for ending abortion. Fifty percent of abortions in America are repeat abortions. If women and men do not receive forgiveness and healing after their first abortion, it's easier for them to fall into a destructive pattern of repeat abortions. If the Church will rise up and cultivate not only a culture of life, but also a culture of healing then we will see an army of the redeemed arise. They will have the authority to speak the truth about abortion, and they will have a heart of wisdom and compassion to open those prison doors and to set the captives free. Together we can help the Bride make herself ready for His return.

Made in the USA
Las Vegas, NV
13 January 2024

84325938R00021